American Lives

Meriwether Lewis

Elizabeth Raum

Heinemann Library
Chicago, Illinois

6/08

© 2004 Heinemann Library
a division of Reed Elsevier Inc.
Chicago, Illinois

Customer Service 888-454-2279

Visit our website at www.heinemannlibrary.com

Designed by Sarah Figlio
Photo research by Alan Gottlieb
Printed in China

08 07
10 9 8 7 6 5 4 3

**Library of Congress
Cataloging-in-Publication Data**
Raum, Elizabeth.
  Meriwether Lewis / by Elizabeth Raum.
    v. cm. -- (American lives)
Includes bibliographical references (p.) and index.
Contents: Brave little hunter -- Child of the Revolution -- School days-- Planter and soldier -- President's secretary -- Planner -- Explorer -- Peace maker -- Grizzly bears and mountains -- Pacific Ocean -- Hero-- Governor -- Lewis's last days.
ISBN 1-4034-4193-6 -- ISBN 1-4034-4201-0 (pbk.)
ISBN 978-1-4034-4193-5 (HC)
ISBN 978-1-4034-4201-7 (Pbk)
1. Lewis, Meriwether, 1774-1809--Juvenile literature. 2.Explorers--West (U.S.)--Biography--Juvenile literature. 3. Lewis and Clark Expedition (1804-1806)--Juvenile literature. 4. West (U.S.)--Discovery and exploration--Juvenile literature. 5. West (U.S.)--Biography--Juvenile literature. [1. Lewis, Meriwether, 1774-1809. 2. Explorers. 3. West (U.S.)--Discovery and exploration.] I. Title. II. American lives (Heinemann Library (Firm)) F592.7.L42R38 2003
  917.804'2'092--dc21
                                      2003004975

Acknowledgments
The author and publishers are grateful to the following for permission to reproduce copyright material: Title page, pp. 5, 11 Independence National Historical Park, Philadelphia; p. 4 Culver Pictures; pp. 7, 9, 23 Bettmann/Corbis; p. 8 North Wind Picture Archives; p. 10 Michael Haynes Historic Art; p. 12 Louis Archambualt, artist, Helena Montana, www.members.aol.com/injwif; p. 13 Library of Congress/Neg.#LC-USZC4-2970; p. 14 National Archives; p. 15 Hulton Archive/Getty Images; p. 16 Smithsonian American Art Museum/Washington, DC/Art Resource, NY; p. 17 National Museum of Wildlife Art, Jackson, Wyoming; p. 18T Oregon Historical Society, neg. #OrHi 101538; p. 18B Oregon Historical Society, neg. #OrHi 101540; pp. 19, 21 Gilcrease Museum; p. 20 Clymer Museum of Art; p. 22 Idaho State Historical Society, neg. # 2715; p. 24 Courtesy American Antiquarian Society; p. 25 American Philosophical Society; p. 26 Missouri Historical Society, St. Louis; p. 27 Missouri Historical Society, St. Louis, photograph by Cary Horton; p. 28 Burstein Collection/Corbis; p. 29 Bobby Mays/Corbis

Cover photograph by Independence National Historical Park, Philadelphia

The author thanks Sheldon Green, her friend and colleague at Concordia College, Moorhead, Minnesota, for sharing his expertise about the journeys of Lewis and Clark.

The publisher would like to thank Michelle Rimsa for her comments in the preparation of this book.

Every effort has been made to contact copyright holders of any material reproduced in this book. Any omissions will be rectified in subsequent printings if notice is given to the publisher.

Some words are shown in bold, **like this.** You can find out what they mean by looking in the glossary.

For more information on the image of Meriwether Lewis that appears on the cover of this book, turn to page 9.

Contents

Brave Little Hunter

When he was only eight years old, Meriwether would go hunting in the middle of the night. That was the best time to catch raccoons and opossums. Meriwether would take his guns and his dogs and head into the forest. Not even snow or cold could stop young Meriwether if he decided to do something. Everyone who knew him agreed that Meriwether was a brave boy.

Meriwether's skills as a young boy led to a lifetime of great adventures.

Years later, President Thomas Jefferson sent Meriwether on a journey across North America. On the journey, Meriwether met many Native American people. He wrote about animals and plants that were unknown to people in the eastern United States. The trip was filled with many dangers, but Meriwether bravely faced each problem.

Meriwether Lewis has been called "the greatest pathfinder this country has ever known."

Child of the Revolution

Meriwether Lewis was born on August 18, 1774, in Albemarle County, near Charlottesville, Virginia. His father, William Lewis, owned a large **plantation** called Locust Hill. As a boy, Meriwether watched **estate** workers growing vegetables, cutting trees, making cloth, and caring for farm animals.

There were few trained doctors in Virginia in the 1700s. Meriwether's mother, Lucy Meriwether Lewis, knew which plants and **herbs** made good medicine. She taught Meriwether how to use herbs to cure sickness.

Lucy Meriwether Lewis was a good mother to her son.

The Life of Meriwether Lewis

1774	1794	1801	1804
Born on August 18, in Albemarle County, Virginia	Became a soldier	Became President Jefferson's secretary	Left on **expedition**

6

The **Revolutionary War** began in 1775. On July 4, 1776, the United States **declared** its freedom from Britain. William Lewis, Meriwether's father, joined the army and was away for the next several years. When Meriwether was five years old, his father died in the war. The plantation went to Meriwether, the oldest son. But he was too young to manage a big plantation. His uncle ran it for him.

This is the cabin that now stands at Lewis's birthplace.

Thomas Jefferson

Thomas Jefferson was a neighbor and friend of the Lewis family when they lived in Virginia. Jefferson, who became the third president of the United States, knew and liked young Meriwether.

1805	1806	1807	1809
Reached the Pacific Ocean	*Returned to St. Louis in September*	*Appointed* ***governor*** *of Louisiana* ***Territory***	*Died on October 11*

7

School Days

Meriwether's mother cared about books and education. She made sure that Meriwether attended school. At home, he learned good manners and how to dance. When Meriwether was eight or nine years old, his stepfather, Captain John Marks, moved the family to northeastern Georgia. It was in Georgia that Meriwether learned how to live in the wilderness. Once, when he was hunting with some friends, an angry bull rushed at them. While his friends looked on, Meriwether raised his gun and killed the bull. His bravery and quick thinking saved their lives.

Young boys only went to school for a few years before taking over chores and responsibilities at home.

When he was about thirteen, Meriwether returned to Virginia. He lived with his Uncle Nicholas, who had been taking care of Locust Hill. Now it was time for Meriwether to learn how to manage the **plantation.** Meriwether and his cousin, Peachy Gilmer, went to school together. They learned math, **botany,** and **geography.** Peachy later said that Meriwether was stubborn, quick to anger, and brave.

Meriwether experienced a lot of change in his young life. He often had to help take care of his family.

Four years later, when Meriwether's stepfather died, his mother decided to live with her family in Virginia. Seventeen-year-old Meriwether left school to help her move.

9

Planter and Soldier

Once he and his mother returned to Virginia, Meriwether took over running Locust Hill. He was good at managing the **plantation.** He grew tobacco and vegetables and raised farm animals. He enjoyed dancing and visiting with friends, but soon became bored with the daily work of running a large farm. Meriwether was pleased when his mother was able to take over.

Meriwether joined the U.S. Army in 1794 and served in a special rifle company.

William Clark was a captain in the U.S. Army. Meriwether was assigned to Clark's unit.

When President George Washington called for help to stop the **Whiskey Rebellion** in western Pennsylvania, twenty-year-old Meriwether volunteered. Army life pleased him. He liked travel, and he enjoyed being a leader. He began as a **private,** but was soon **promoted.** Eventually he became a captain. While Meriwether was in the army, he met William Clark, who later became his partner in exploring the West.

President's Secretary

Thomas Jefferson was elected president of the United States in 1801. Jefferson needed someone he could trust to be his secretary. He had heard that his young neighbor Meriwether Lewis was in the army. When the president asked Meriwether to be his secretary, Lewis agreed. As the president's secretary, Lewis gathered information for Thomas Jefferson, and he carried reports and messages to **Congress.** Lewis lived in the President's House.

President Jefferson and Lewis planned the expedition together at Monticello, Jefferson's home in Virginia.

The President's House

The home of the U.S. President has had several names, including the President's House, the President's Palace, and the Executive Mansion. President Theodore Roosevelt named it the White House in 1901.

Lewis studied with people from the University of Pennsylvania and gathered information about a possible route for the journey.

In the evenings, President Jefferson and Lewis talked about the future of the United States. Jefferson said that he wanted to send an explorer west across North America to map a trail from the Mississippi River to the Pacific Ocean. The president wanted to learn about the land and the plants and animals of the West. He also wanted information about the Native Americans who lived there. Lewis was eager to make the trip. Jefferson agreed that Lewis was the right man to lead an **expedition.**

Planner

Lewis and the president began planning for the **expedition.** They talked about how many people to take, what boats and supplies to bring, and what gifts to bring for the Native Americans. Jefferson asked Lewis to keep a journal and to treat Native Americans kindly. Lewis prepared for the trip by learning **botany** so he could describe plants, **astronomy** so he could find his way using the stars, and medicine so that he could help his people if they got sick.

Lewis's journals listed the gifts brought by the explorers for the Native Americans they met.

Louisiana Purchase

*On April 30, 1803, the United States purchased 828,000 square miles (more than a million square kilometers) of land from France. This was called the **Louisiana Purchase.** Lewis and Clark explored part of the Louisiana Purchase.*

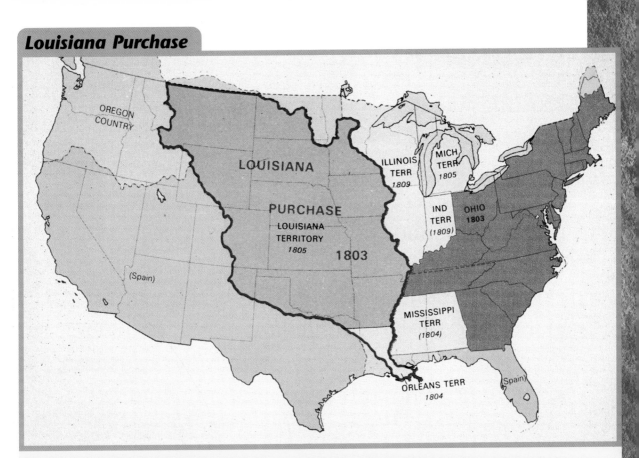

The purchase of the Louisiana Territory doubled the size of the United States. However, it needed to be explored to find out what was there and how far the territory actually went. Lewis and his men explored, scouted, **surveyed,** and mapped the lands of the Louisiana Purchase.

Lewis wrote to his army friend William Clark, asking him to help lead the expedition. Clark was a soldier and mapmaker. The two men trusted one another. Lewis promised Clark that they would both be captains and lead the expedition together. Clark agreed to go.

Explorer

Existing maps stopped at the Mandan villages near present-day Bismarck, North Dakota. Lewis would have to figure out the rest of the way to the Pacific Ocean. Lewis had little information about the people and places along the way. Fur traders told strange stories of woolly mammoths who roamed the prairies, giants who spoke strange languages, and mountains made of salt. Native Americans also gave them some information about what lay beyond. Lewis did not know what he would discover on the way west.

The Missouri River was shallow and muddy when Lewis used it to travel north on the **expedition.**

Seaman

Lewis bought a dog for the trip. Seaman was a black Newfoundland who was a good swimmer. He helped the expedition by hunting squirrels, geese, and beavers. Sometimes Seaman kept Lewis awake at night because he barked when he heard bears.

On May 21, 1804, Lewis and the explorers left St. Charles, Missouri. Travel on the Missouri River was dangerous, but they made good progress. They hunted deer, turkey, geese, and elk. They camped at the river's edge. They saw prairie dogs, coyotes, and pronghorn antelopes. These animals were unknown to scientists in the eastern part of the country.

Mosquitoes were a constant problem for the team. Mosquitoes were especially dangerous because they carried a disease called **malaria.** Many of the men, including Lewis, caught this disease.

Lewis liked prairie dogs so much that he shipped a live one to President Jefferson.

Peacemaker

Whenever Lewis met Native American chiefs, he gave a speech about peace and informed them about the **Louisiana Purchase.** He gave them peace medals as a gift from President Jefferson. Throughout the trip, Native Americans helped Lewis by giving him directions, food, shelter, horses, and boats. Without this help, the **expedition** would have failed.

Lewis often went wandering in the woods alone. He liked to be by himself and to look for new plants, animals, and birds.

Lewis gave peace medals like these to all the Native American chiefs he saw in Missouri.

Lewis brought many gifts for the Native Americans, including clothes, tobacco, paint, knives, and beads.

In October 1804, the Mandan welcomed Lewis to their villages. The Mandan villages were a major trading center. Lewis visited them to learn about the Mandan people.

At Fort Mandan, Lewis met Toussaint Charbonneau, a fur trader, and his Shoshoni wife, Sacagawea. The Charbonneaus asked to go west with him. Lewis agreed. He hired Charbonneau to act as an **interpreter.** Lewis hoped Sacagawea would ask the Shoshoni people to sell him some horses to carry men and supplies across the Rocky Mountains.

Grizzly Bears and Mountains

On April 7, 1805, the **expedition** left the Mandan villages. They saw huge herds of buffalo. Lewis and his men were chased by a grizzly bear. Lewis killed the bear, but it took several bullets.

One day in August, Lewis was wandering alone when he met some Shoshoni. They took him to their chief, Cameahwait, who was Sacagawea's brother. Cameahwait agreed to sell 29 horses to Lewis.

Lewis and his men ran into many wild animals during their trip. They had to fight to stay alive.

On May 26, 1805, Lewis saw the Rocky Mountains for the first time.

The trip across the Rocky Mountains was very difficult because of heavy snow. The men had no food and were so hungry that they had to kill and eat one of the horses. When they finally left the mountains, they met Native Americans who gave them food and shelter. Lewis became very ill after eating too much of the food. Lewis and the men rested until they were well enough to travel again.

Pacific Ocean

On the other side of the Rocky Mountains, the explorers found a beautiful valley and rivers full of fish. With the help of the **Nez Percé,** they built and sailed canoes down the Clearwater River to the Snake River and finally to the Columbia River. There were plenty of fish to eat, especially salmon, but the men soon got tired of fish. Lewis bought dogs from a local tribe and cooked them for his team.

The Nez Percé had never seen white men before the **expedition** arrived. According to tribal history, the Nez Percé had to decide between killing or being friendly to the strangers.

Since there were no maps to show the way, Lewis and Clark did not know how to get to the Pacific Ocean. Lewis went ahead with a small group of men. He reached the ocean on November 14, 1805. A few days later, when Clark and his group went out, they found Lewis's name carved in a tree near the shore. Clark added the date to the tree carving.

Lewis's abilities as a leader and explorer helped him successfully lead 40 men over land to the Pacific Ocean.

President Jefferson had hoped that Lewis could take a ship home. All winter Lewis searched the shore for ships, but none ever came. He and his team had to return over land.

Hero

On March 23, 1806, the **expedition** headed home. When Lewis and Clark arrived in St. Louis, Missouri, on September 23, 1806, people cheered and called them heroes. There were parties and parades. Lewis made his way to Locust Hill to see his mother. Then he traveled to Washington, D.C., to meet with President Jefferson. Lewis spent the winter in the President's House in Washington. People gave dinners in Lewis's honor, and he told them about his daring adventures.

This newspaper article announced the arrival of Lewis and his men in St. Louis.

By the last Mails.

MARYLAND.

BALTIMORE, OCT. 29, 1806.

A LETTER from *St. Louis (Upper Louisiana),* dated *Sept.* 23, 1806, announces the arrival of Captains LEWIS and CLARK, from their expedition into the interior.—They went to the *Pacific Ocean;* have brought some of the natives and curiosities of the countries through which they passed, and only lost one man. They left the *Pacific Ocean* 23d March, 1806, where they arrived in November, 1805;—and where some American vessels had been just before.—They state the Indians to be as numerous on the *Columbia* river, which empties into the *Pacific,* as the whites in any part of the U. S. They brought a family of the Mandan indians with them. The winter was very mild on the *Pacific.*— They have kept an ample journal of their tour; which will be published, and must afford much intelligence.

While in Washington, D.C., Lewis made sure that his men were given land and money as a reward for going on the expedition. He also worked on the notes that he had made during the trip. The president wanted Lewis to **publish** the journals so that everyone could read about his adventures. However, Lewis never finished them.

President Jefferson had asked Lewis to take careful notes of everything he saw during the journey. This picture in Lewis's journal is of a white salmon trout.

Life After the Expedition

In 1807, President Jefferson appointed Lewis **governor** of the Louisiana **Territory.** Before he left Washington, D.C., Lewis wrote a paper about the fur trade. He also traveled to Virginia where he hoped to find a wife. He met many young women, but he never married.

Lewis's Firsts

Lewis was the first American explorer to:

- *describe or draw over 100 kinds of birds and animals*
- *describe or draw over 200 kinds of plants*
- *meet and describe over 50 groups of Native American peoples*

In the late 1800s, St. Louis was a leading transportation and trade center because of its location on the Missouri and Mississippi Rivers.

The watch that Lewis took with him on the **expedition** can be seen at the Missouri Historical Society Museum in St. Louis.

Lewis tried to be a good governor, but he missed exploring. He worked with Native American chiefs to bring about peace. He met with important people, built roads, and began projects to make the territory a better place.

He moved alone to St. Louis in 1808. When Lewis heard that William Clark and his wife were moving to St. Louis, he found them a home. Lewis ate many meals with the Clarks. When the Clarks had a baby boy, they named him Meriwether Lewis Clark in honor of their good friend.

Lewis's Last Days

Lewis saw a bright future for the Louisiana **Territory.** He bought land and went into business with a fur trading company. Lewis worked hard to keep the peace. It cost a lot of money to pay soldiers, buy supplies, and build **forts.** When he asked government officials in Washington, D.C., for money to pay some of the bills, they said no. Lewis was very upset. He decided to go to Washington, D.C., to speak with the new U.S. president, James Madison.

When Lewis and his team came upon the three forks of the Missouri River, Lewis named one of the rivers the Madison, in honor of President James Madison.

The Journals

Lewis's journals were published in 1814, several years after he died. The journals proved to the world that Lewis was a great American hero.

Lewis started out on the journey to Washington, D.C. He never made it there. He died of a gunshot wound on October 11, 1809, in Tennessee. He was only 35 years old.

Lewis's sudden death saddened many people, especially William Clark and Thomas Jefferson, the people who knew him best. Meriwether Lewis had been a strong leader who loved his country and faced danger bravely.

Lewis is buried at Meriwether Lewis Park in Hohenwald, Tennessee.

Glossary

astronomy study of the stars

botany study of plants

Congress part of U.S. government that makes the laws

declare say clearly or announce

estate fine country house on a large piece of land

expedition journey taken for a special purpose

fort strong building used for defense against enemy attack

geography study of places

governor person who is in charge of a state or territory

herb plant used as medicine

interpreter person who explains what someone is saying in another language

Louisiana Purchase western half of the Mississippi River basin purchased in 1803 from France by the United States

malaria disease that causes chills and fevers

Nez Percé member of a Native American people of Idaho, Washington, and Oregon

plantation large estate with many workers

private person of low rank in the military

promote give a more important job

publish make into a book for readers

Revolutionary War war from 1775 to 1783 in which the American colonists won freedom from Great Britain

survey measure and map land

territory part of the United States that is not yet a state

Whiskey Rebellion uprising against taxes on liquor

More Books to Read

DeVillier, Christy. *Lewis & Clark*. Edina, Minn.: ABDO, 2001.

Herbert, Janis. *Lewis and Clark for Kids*. Chicago: Chicago Review Press, 2000.

Isaacs, Sally Senzell. *America in the Time of Lewis and Clark*. Chicago: Heinemann Library, 1999.

Johmann, Carol A. *The Lewis and Clark Expedition*. Charlotte, Vt.: Williamson Publishing, 2002.

Patent, Dorothy Hinshaw. *Animals on the Trail with Lewis and Clark*. New York: Clarion, 2002.

Places to Visit

Fort Clatsop National Memorial (reconstructed fort)
92343 Fort Clatsop Road
Astoria, Oregon 97103
Visitor Information: (503) 861-2471

Jefferson National Expansion Memorial
11 North 4th Street
St. Louis, Missouri 63102
Visitor Information: (314) 655-1700

The North Dakota Lewis & Clark Interpretive Center
P.O. Box 607
Washburn, ND 58577-0607
Visitor Information: (701) 462-8535

Index

W9-BQS-078

★ IT'S MY STATE! ★
Maryland

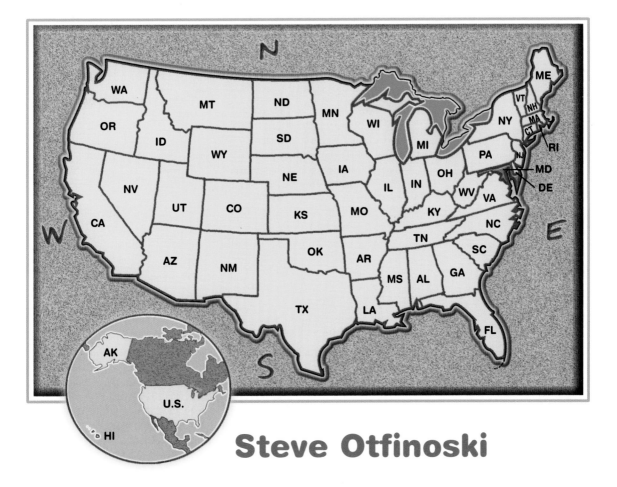

Steve Otfinoski

BENCHMARK BOOKS

MARSHALL CAVENDISH
NEW YORK

Series Consultant

David G. Vanderstel, Ph.D., Executive Director, National Council on Public History

With thanks to Joe and Sue Swisher

Benchmark Books
Marshall Cavendish
99 White Plains Road
Tarrytown, New York 10591-9001
www.marshallcavendish.com

Library of Congress Cataloging-in-Publication Data

Otfinoski, Steve.
Maryland / by Steve Otfinoski.
p. cm. — (It's my state!)
Summary: Surveys the history, geography, government, and economy of the
Old Line State as well as the diverse ways of life of its people.
Includes bibliographical references and index.
ISBN 0-7614-1421-5
1. Maryland—Juvenile literature. [1. Maryland.] I. Title. II.
Series.
F181.3 .O84 2003
975.2—dc21
2002002706

Photo research by Candlepants, Inc.

Cover Photo: *Richard T. Nowitz / Corbis*

Back cover illustration: The license plate shows Maryland's postal abbreviation, followed by its year of statehood.

The photographs in this book are used by permission and through the courtesy of: *Photo Researchers, Inc.*: Maslowski, 4 (middle); M. E. Warren, 4 (bottom); Jeff Lepore, 13, 16 (middle), 17 (middle); Andrew J. Martinez, 5 (middle); L. West, 5 (bottom); Rod Planck, 17 (bottom); Michael P. Gadomski, 19. *Corbis*: 36, 50 (bottom); Bettmann, 31, 38, 41 (top), 41 (bottom), 50 (top), 50 (middle), 51 (top), 51 (middle); AFP, 51 (bottom), 72 (bottom); Paul A. Souders, 8, 12, 42, 53, 54, 56, 58, 62, 68; Catherine Karnow, 9; Dale C. Spartas, 5 (top), 14; David Muench, 10, 11, 16 (top); Raymond Gehman, 16 (bottom), 17, (top); Kevin Fleming, 18, 60, 67; The Mariner's Museum, 22; Lee Snider, 28; Underwood & Underwood, 32; Ed Eckstein, 45; Richard T. Nowitz, 46, 48, 49, 69, 73 (middle), 73 (bottom); Lowell Georgia, 57, 63, 64, 72 (top); Robert Maass, 52; Roger Ressmeyer, 66; James L. Amos, 71, 73 (top). *Picture Quest*: Stockbyte, 72 (middle). *Art Resource, NY / Scala*: 34. *Maryland Historical Society Baltimore, Maryland*: 26, 30, 33, 39. *Maryland State Archives SPECIAL COLLECTIONS (Maryland Commission on Artistic Property) Painting of George Calvert, by J.A. Vintner (MSA SC 1545-1101):* 23. *Dan Beigel:* 4 (top), 74.

Book design by Anahid Hamparian

Printed in Italy

1   3   5   6   4   2

Contents

A Quick Look at Maryland

Nickname: The Free State or the Old Line State
Population: 5,296,486 (2000)
Statehood: 1788

Flower: Black-Eyed Susan

This small wildflower is also called the yellow daisy. It is hard to pick the flower without pulling the plant up by the roots because the stems are so tough.

Bird: Baltimore Oriole

The male oriole's black and orange feathers are the colors of the coat of arms of the Calverts, the English family that founded Maryland. The Baltimore Orioles baseball team is named for this bird.

Tree: White Oak

The most famous white oak in Maryland was the Wye Oak. It was one of the largest oak trees in the world and was more than 450 years old. The Wye Oak was recently destroyed by a storm.

Dog: Chesapeake Bay Retriever

Maryland's state dog is very special. It is one of the few dog breeds native to the United States. It got its name because it is trained to retrieve game birds shot by hunters.

Fish: Rockfish

This fish is also known as the striped bass. It can be identified by the seven or eight dark stripes running from its head to its tail.

Insect: Baltimore Checkerspot Butterfly

The colorful checkerspot, like other butterflies, lays its eggs on only one plant—the turtlehead, a member of the snapdragon family.

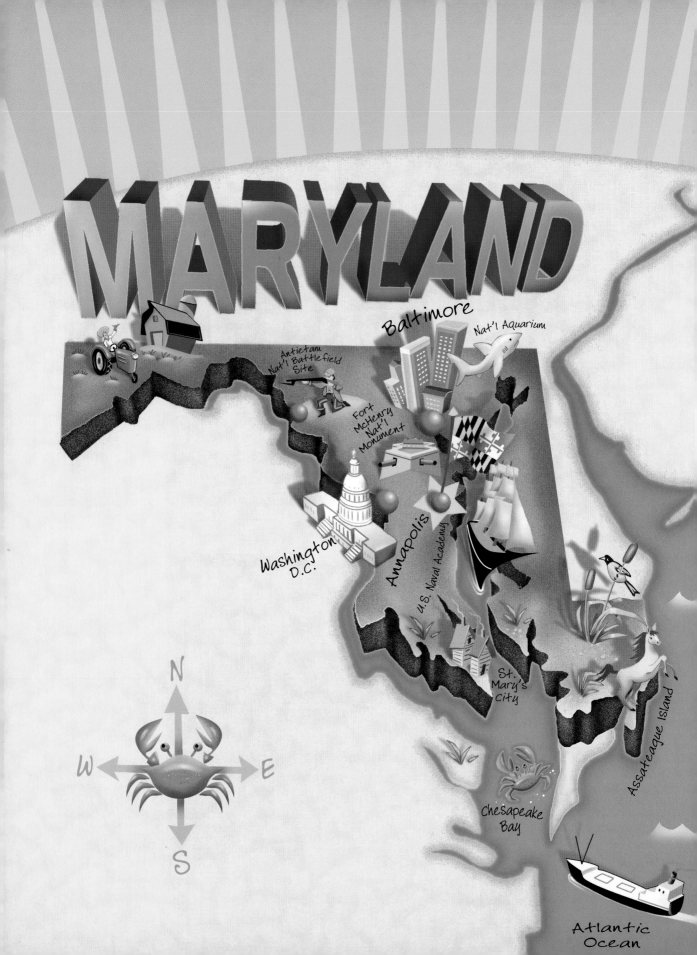

1 The Free State

Maryland is the ninth-smallest state. For such a small state, it has a lot of people. Maryland's population was 5,296,486 in 2000. That makes it the nineteenth most populous state. Maryland has a lot to attract all these people—plains, hills, valleys, mountains, and ocean beaches. Forests cover two-fifths of the state. About 150 different kinds of trees thrive here. Maryland also has one of the finest bays in the world—the Chesapeake Bay. Maryland has it all.

The Chesapeake Bay

Wherever you go in Maryland, you are never very far from water. The Chesapeake Bay nearly cuts the state in half. Only thirty-one miles of the state face the Atlantic Ocean. The Chesapeake Bay, however, provides Maryland with a long shoreline that runs 3,190 miles. The bay has many good harbors for boats. The region to the east of the bay is called the Eastern Shore.

Maryland's Borders

North: Pennsylvania
South: District of Columbia
East: Delaware and the Atlantic Ocean
West: West Virginia and Virginia

7

Schooners racing along the Chesapeake Bay on a clear day

The name Chesapeake Bay comes from the Native American word *Chesepiuk*. Some people say it is the name of an Indian village at the mouth of the bay. Others believe it means "great shellfish bay." Either meaning fits the Chesapeake. Since Native American times, people have been catching oysters, crabs, and fish in its clear blue waters.

Most of Maryland's twenty-three major rivers flow into the Chesapeake Bay or the Atlantic Ocean. Maryland has twenty-three counties. Sixteen of them border the Chesapeake shore.

There are no natural lakes in Maryland. All existing lakes have been

America in miniature—a small state, it offers a large part of the variety of attractions found in the United States as a whole.
—Theodore McKeldin

Maryland's lakes offer a variety of activities for the state's residents.

made artificially by damming rivers. The largest of these, Deep Creek Lake, is twelve miles long.

Marylanders enjoy all the water that surrounds them. Some like to sail their boats in the bay, while others prefer to water ski. Sport fishing is popular in the Atlantic Ocean, and many enjoy catching crabs in the bay and rivers.

Plains, Plateaus, and Mountains

Maryland's varied landscape is divided into three land regions. The most eastern part—which is almost split into two parts by the Chesapeake Bay—is called the Coastal Plain. The area is riddled with marshes and swamps. Much of the fertile land is used for growing crops and raising chickens. The Coastal Plain is home to Baltimore, Maryland's largest city. Ocean City, a popular beach town, is also located there. While only 5,000 residents live there year-round, as many as 250,000 tourists visit each summer.

Beyond the plains region stretches a wide area called the Piedmont Plateau. The plateau's hills and valleys contain most of the state's dairy farms.

The Appalachian Region with its two mountain ranges—the Alleghenies and Blue Ridge, which are part of the Appalachian Mountains—is located in western Maryland where apple orchards thrive in the cooler weather and the forests provide many jobs.

The Blue Ridge Mountains extend as far south as northern Georgia and cut across a narrow strip of Maryland. They form

The marshland by the Nassawango Creek on the lower Eastern Shore of Maryland is home to different plants and animals.

A breathtaking view of the Blue Ridge Mountains

one of the loveliest corners of the state. Their name comes from the blue haze that appears to hang over the mountains. The Appalachians were formed close to 230 million years ago by disturbances in the earth's crust. They are the oldest mountains in North America. At Hancock, Maryland, in the Appalachian Region, the state is less than two miles wide from north to south. This is the narrowest width recorded in any state. The Allegheny Mountains, which are part of the Appalachian Mountains, are there. At 3,360 feet, Backbone Mountain is the highest peak in Maryland.

Climate

Eastern Maryland can thank the Gulf Stream for its mild climate.

Marylanders can have fun cooling down in Ocean City, which is right on the shore of the Atlantic Ocean.

The Gulf Stream is a warm ocean current that flows north from the Gulf of Mexico. In the summer, however, Eastern Maryland can be hot and humid. The mountainous region in the western part of the state is considerably cooler and gets the most snowfall in the state. Up to seventy-eight inches of snow can fall there every year. The state receives an average of forty-four inches of rain a year. That's a lot of rain!

Violent storms and hurricanes are rare in Maryland. An exception was Hurricane Agnes which struck the Maryland coast in 1972. It caused $110 million in damage and took nineteen lives.

Animals—Tame and Wild

Maryland once had large wild animals such as elk and buffalo. But hunters have killed most of them. The rest have been driven away by people. The only big mammal that is left in large numbers is the white-tailed deer. Only a few black bears still wander through the western mountains. If you walk through wooded areas, you'll come upon many smaller animals, though—raccoons, muskrats, gray squirrels, and red foxes.

The Chesapeake Bay's marshes are home to thousands of water birds. They include all kinds of ducks and Canada geese. The great blue heron lives near the state's many rivers and streams, where it catches fish. With its

Some Canada geese can have wingspans of more than six feet.

long pointed bill and thin storklike legs, it is the largest American heron. Maryland hunters stalk game birds such as quail, mourning doves, and ring-necked pheasants.

Hunters often use Maryland's state dog, the Chesapeake Bay retriever, to find the game birds they have shot. No one

The loyal Chesapeake Bay retriever can easily run on land and swim in the water.

knows for sure how this dog breed developed in Maryland. One story goes that an English ship was wrecked off the coast in the early 1800s. Two Newfoundland dogs were saved from the ship. They were bred with local dogs. Over time, they produced a new breed.

Bay retrievers are highly intelligent and very loyal dogs. Sometimes they are trained to smell out drugs for law enforcement officers and to perform rescue work. These dogs are so friendly that they are brought to hospitals and nursing homes to cheer up patients.

Marylanders have not had as good a relationship with their state bird, the Baltimore oriole. The oriole was given protection under state law in 1882 and was further protected under the state's Nongame and Endangered Species Conservation Act in 1975. Despite this, the bird's population has been declining. Much of its habitat has been destroyed by the construction of offices, stores, and factories. Also, many orioles have died from eating insects containing poisonous pesticides.

The Chesapeake Bay is full of many kinds of fish—such as shad, drumfish, and rockfish—that are fished commercially. In the ocean, sport fishers hook their lines to catch marlins, which resemble swordfish and can weigh up to four hundred pounds. In the rivers and streams, trout and perch are favorite catches. Marshes are home to the diamondback terrapin, Maryland's state reptile. These relatives of turtles are named for the diamond-shaped rings on their upper shell. Before laws were passed to protect them, diamondbacks were nearly hunted into extinction for their delicious meat.

Plants & Animals

Bald Cypress Tree

The bald cypress tree is not really a cypress but a relative of the sequoia (suh-KWOY-uh) tree. The Battle Creek Cypress Swamp Nature Center in southern Maryland has the northernmost stand (area) of bald cypress in the United States. Some of the trees are more than five hundred years old.

Whistling Swan

The whistling swan does not really whistle. Its name refers to the sound made by its wings beating in flight. It is also called the tundra swan.

Great Blue Heron

The great blue heron is the largest kind of heron found in North America. It uses its large pointed bill to catch fish in rivers and streams.

White-Tailed Deer

When the white-tailed deer is frightened, its tail stands straight up, showing its white color. The deer's tail is about a foot long.

Delmarva Fox Squirrel

The Delmarva fox squirrel is one of Maryland's endangered species. This large tree squirrel is shy and quiet. It's not very good at climbing trees and usually runs along the ground when chased by a predator.

Fragrant Water Lily

This sweet-smelling plant is Maryland's only native water lily and has large floating leaves and blossoms with many petals. Native Americans once used different parts of the plants for medicine and food.

The Wild Ponies of Assateague Island

Perhaps Maryland's most intriguing animals are the wild ponies of Assateague Island. This long, narrow island lies off Maryland's Atlantic coast. Two million visitors come to the island each year to see its ponies.

How the ponies got there is a mystery. One legend claims a Spanish ship ran aground on the island many years ago. Horses on board escaped. Many now believe that the horses are descended from work horses that farmers brought to the island and let graze on the marsh grass.

These wild ponies are running along Assateague Island's Atlantic shore.

Scientists hope to preserve all of the wildlife on the island by controlling the population of wild ponies.

The wild ponies still eat the marsh grass today. This has become a problem. The marsh grass holds the sand together to form dunes. If new dunes aren't created, the ocean waters will eat away at the land. One day the island will be covered by water.

Scientists are working on ways to control the wild pony population. State workers shoot darts at the female horses, called mares. The darts contain a vaccine. It prevents the mares from having babies. This will keep the number of ponies down and help protect the island. Each year, some of the ponies are also rounded up and sold at auctions. This also helps to control the pony population there.

There was a certain peaceful satisfaction to seeing horses in the marsh, set against the bay and mainland shore. But to tell the truth, the horses didn't really seem wild. Rather than have to whisper to keep them calm, I thought I would have to shout to get their attention.
—James Gorman

2 From the Beginning

Maryland is the most southern of the middle Atlantic states. It shares features of both the North and the South. It has had divided loyalties going back as far as the Revolutionary War. That means that different groups of people in the state were loyal to different causes. Marylanders have usually met history's challenges with courage and determination.

The First Peoples of Maryland

Native Americans first came to Maryland in about 10,000 B.C. The only traces they left behind were pottery, arrowheads, and burial sites.

By the 1600s, various Algonquian tribes were living along the Chesapeake Bay. The Piscataway and Patuxent peoples lived in southern Maryland. The Choptank, Nanticoke, and Assateague lived on the Eastern Shore. The Susquehanna settled at the head of the bay. Most of these peoples were peaceful. They lived in long huts made from the wood of trees and covered with grass. Villages were small and consisted of only several hundred people. The men fished and gathered shellfish from the bay. The

Maryland children attending Sunday school in the early 1900s

21

The arrival of European explorers and settlers greatly changed the way of life of Maryland's Native Americans.

women grew corn, squash, and tobacco. This simple way of life, however, would soon be challenged by newcomers.

Explorers and Settlers

The Italian explorer Giovanni da Verrazano may have been the first European to see Maryland. He sailed past the Chesapeake Bay in 1524 while exploring the shoreline of America for the king of France. The first explorer to actually visit the area was Englishman John Smith. In 1608, Smith sailed up the Chesapeake Bay. He found Maryland "a delightsome land!"

However, Smith found better possibilities to the south and was one of the colonizers of the Virginia colony. William Claiborne, a member of the Virginia colony, began exploring to the north. He too

[The fish were] lying so thick with their heads above the waters [that] we attempted to catch them with a frying pan.
—Captain John Smith

was attracted to the Chesapeake Bay but saw its potential for colonization. Claiborne set up a trading post on Kent Island in the bay in 1631. This was the state's first permanent settlement.

The next year the English king Charles I granted the region to George Calvert. Calvert, the first Lord Baltimore, died soon afterward. His son Cecilius Calvert received the

George Calvert, the first Lord Baltimore

land grant. He named the colony Maryland after Queen Henrietta Maria. Cecilius's brother Leonard landed in Maryland with two hundred settlers in March 1634. He bought land from the local Native Americans and founded the settlement of St. Mary's City on the Western Shore. The Calverts wanted Maryland to be a safe place for Catholics to settle.

In 1649, the legislature passed the Act Concerning Religion. It gave all Christians living in Maryland the right to choose how they worshiped. It is one of the first laws granting religious freedom in America.

A Model Longhouse

When the first European settlers arrived in Maryland, many of the Native Americans there lived in longhouses. The longhouse frames were made from two rows of thin poles stuck into the ground. The Native Americans bent the rows toward each other and tied each pair of poles together. The frame was covered with bark or woven grass mats. Many people lived in each house. You can make a small model of one of these longhouses.

What You Need

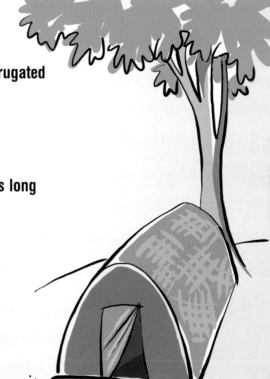

Chinet paper dinner plate or piece of corrugated
      cardboard, about 9 inches square
Plastic wrap (if using cardboard square)
Scotch tape
Brown clay, about 1 cup
Ten brown or tan pipe cleaners, 12 inches long
Ruler
Scissors
Brown paper bag
Water
Red or yellow paper

If using a cardboard square, cover it with plastic wrap and tape the plastic wrap down on the back to keep the cardboard dry.

Shape the clay into a ball and place it in the center of the plate or cardboard. Flatten the clay into an oval that is at least 1/4 inch thick.

Cut six pipe cleaners into 8-inch lengths and save the extra pieces.

Bend six of the 8-inch pieces of pipe cleaner into hoops, with two straight sides and a curved top (like an upside down U). Line them up one behind the other, about a finger-width apart, with both ends sticking into the clay. Attach a long piece across the tops of the hoops. Secure it by twisting both ends of the pipe cleaner around the tops of the first and last hoops. Do the same with two long pieces, placing each on both sides of the first one, about an inch away. For extra support you can cut small pieces of pipe cleaner and attach them across the ends of the hoops.

Cut a piece of brown paper bag to fit over the top of the long-house, from the ground on one side to the ground on the other. Cut two more pieces to cover the ends. Make sure they are the same size and shape as the ends of the longhouse. Cut a doorway in one of the end pieces.

To make the paper look more like bark or grass, crumple it, wet it, then flatten it out. Lay the biggest piece over the longhouse top so it dries in the shape you want. When the paper is dry, tape the top to the end pieces by attaching a piece of tape to the inside of the long piece, so that about an inch of tape hangs off the end. Hold one of the end pieces of paper in place. Attach the end piece by using the tape that is hanging off the end of the long piece. This way the tape will not show. Repeat these steps for the other end piece. You can use several pieces of tape to make sure the paper stays, but you do not need to tape the paper to the frame.

You can make a "fire" inside the longhouse with tiny bits of pipe cleaner as logs and colored paper as flames.

The Ark *and the* Dove, *the two ships that brought the Calverts and other settlers to Maryland, were well stocked with supplies for the long voyage across the Atlantic Ocean.*

A Growing Colony

Over the years and despite several political disputes with Claiborne about ownership of Kent Island and settlers wanting to govern themselves, the Calvert family ruled the colony of Maryland. In 1689, colonists seized the government and demanded that the king take over the colony. The first royal governor arrived in 1692. Two years later, the capital was moved from St. Mary's to Anne Arundel Town. Later, its name would be changed to Annapolis.

Maryland farmers built tobacco plantations along the rivers that empty into the Chesapeake Bay. They needed many workers for these big farms. In 1664, slavery became legal in the colony. African slaves were brought to Maryland by ship. But until the 1680s, the colony also had free blacks and both black and white indentured servants. These were people whose passage to America was paid in exchange for work for a master for up to seven years. After that the servant was freed. Mathias de Sousa was a black indentured servant who arrived with the first colonists on *The Ark* in 1634. He soon gained his freedom and became the first African American to serve in the state's general assembly in 1642.

By the 1680s, there were few white indentured servants. More and more slaves were brought in to take their places on the large tobacco plantations. Most of the slaves led miserable lives, working long hours six days a week. They lived in shabby cabins and ate practically inedible food.

I have no patriotism. I have no country. What country have I? . . . I am not thought of, spoken of, except as a piece of property belonging to some Christian slaveholder, and all the religious and political institutions of this country alike pronounce me a slave. . .

—Frederick Douglass, who grew up enslaved in Maryland and later fought for the rights of African Americans

The colony continued to grow. During the 1700s, European settlers forced many Native Americans to move west, out of Maryland. Some Native Americans were killed when they refused to give up their land. Others died of diseases brought by the settlers from Europe. Today only about five thousand Native Americans live in the state.

The city of Baltimore, founded in 1729, became a center where farmers could sell their goods. In the 1760s, Maryland quarreled with Pennsylvania over its border. England sent two surveyors, Charles Mason and Jeremiah Dixon, to draw up the boundary line between the two colonies. In 1767, they completed the Mason-Dixon Line. To this day, the Mason-Dixon Line marks the border between northern and southern states.

This stone marker still stands at the Mason-Dixon Line.

Maryland

The First and Second American Revolutions

A larger conflict was growing between England and its American colonies. While tobacco farmers and some other Marylanders were on good terms with the British, many colonists wanted independence from England. In 1774, Maryland patriots in Annapolis copied the Boston Tea Party of 1773. They protested the British tax on tea by burning a British ship, the *Peggy Stewart*, and its cargo of tea.

Some historians believe that George Washington himself gave Maryland its first nickname, the Old Line State. Washington was greatly impressed with the Maryland Line, its regular line troops. They fought courageously in the Revolution. Today Maryland is still called the Old Line State.

War broke out in April 1775. Not much fighting took place in Maryland. Maryland soldiers, however, fought bravely in many battles.

The Americans won their independence in 1783. The thirteen colonies—now states—struggled to find a new form of government. In September 1786, Annapolis hosted a states' convention. Delegates discussed the issues of trade and business. They agreed to meet again in Philadelphia in 1788.

At the Philadelphia convention, a Constitution was written. This was a bold plan for a national government. Maryland became the seventh state to ratify, or approve, the new Constitution on April 28, 1788.

In 1812, England once again went to war with America. People sometimes call the War of 1812 the second American Revolution. This time much of the fighting took place in Maryland. In 1813, the British raided towns along Chesapeake

Troops preparing to defend Baltimore during the War of 1812

Bay. In September 1814, they attacked Baltimore. American lawyer Francis Scott Key was aboard a British boat waiting for the release of a friend who was a British prisoner. From the boat, he watched the British bombard Fort McHenry in the Baltimore harbor. All day and night, Key watched the British ship fire 1,800 rockets, bombs, and shells at the fort.

To Key's joy, the American flag still flew over the fort "in the dawn's early light." The British retreated. On the way to shore, Key began to write a poem about the event.

Less than a week later, his poem, "Defense of Fort McHenry," was published in a Baltimore newspaper. It was later set to the tune of an old English song and became "The Star-Spangled Banner." In 1931, eighty-eight years after Key's

Francis Scott Key observing Fort McHenry from the Baltimore harbor

From the Beginning

death, his patriotic song officially became our national anthem.

The British were driven back from Baltimore and from New York State later that fall. A peace treaty was signed in December 1814.

The Civil War

The 1800s saw Maryland make great strides in industry and development. The first national highway, called the National Road, was built in 1818. It joined Cumberland, Maryland, with Wheeling, West Virginia. Peter Cooper built one of the first American steam locomotives, which made its initial run in 1830. The first ocean-going iron steamship was completed in Baltimore in 1839. In 1844, the first message was sent over a telegraph line between Baltimore and Washington, D.C.

Peter Cooper's steam locomotive, the Tom Thumb, *making its first run in 1830*

Maryland

Maryland soldiers beside their cannon during the Civil War

All these achievements helped bring Americans closer together, but the issue of slavery moved them farther apart. The North opposed slavery, and the South supported it. Harriet Tubman, a runaway slave from Maryland, helped many other slaves escape from the South. She led them to the North and Canada using the Underground Railroad, a system that used safe routes and people who were willing to hide slaves in their "friendly" homes en route to freedom.

I was the conductor of the Underground Railroad for eight years, and I can say what most conductors can't say—I never ran my train off the track and I never lost a passenger.
— Harriet Tubman

In early 1861, a number of Southern states seceded, or broke away, from the Union. Some 14,000 slaveholders in Maryland wanted their state to secede and join the Southern Confederacy. Other residents wanted Maryland to remain in the Union, and it did. However, on April 19, 1861, a mob of pro-Confederates attacked Massachusetts's troops, which were traveling through Baltimore. Four soldiers and twelve other people died. It was the first violence of the soon-to-come Civil War.

More than 70,000 Maryland soldiers fought in the war. About 50,000 of them fought for the Union. Several important battles were fought in the state. The biggest was the Battle of Antietam on September 17, 1862.

The North called the bloodiest battle of the Civil War the Battle of Antietam, after the nearby creek, but the South called it the Battle of Sharpsburg, after the Maryland town.

Maryland

Confederate General Robert E. Lee had invaded Maryland with 50,000 troops two weeks earlier. Under General George McClellan, 90,000 Union soldiers met them at Antietam Creek. The fighting began in the early morning. It continued throughout the day. When it ended, more than 23,000 were dead or wounded. That is twice the number of soldiers killed in the War of 1812, the Mexican War, and the Spanish-American War combined. It was the single bloodiest day of the Civil War.

> *Men are falling in their places or running back into the corn. Many of the recruits who are killed or wounded only left home ten days ago.*
>
> —A Union soldier at Antietam

Lee retreated to Virginia. The Union declared victory. It was an expensive victory, but it did strengthen the North's position. It also led President Abraham Lincoln to prepare his famous Emancipation Proclamation, which freed the slaves in the Confederate states.

In 1864, Maryland adopted a new constitution that abolished slavery. It also punished people who supported the Confederacy. The war ended in Union victory the following year.

Growth and Reform

In the years following the Civil War, Maryland became a leader in science and education. Johns Hopkins University was founded in Baltimore in 1876. The world-famous Johns Hopkins Hospital opened thirteen years later. The hospital and school

Many young children had to work in dangerous and unhealthy conditions to help support their families. This boy worked in a packing plant in Baltimore.

today remain important research centers. Johns Hopkins's doctors have discovered new treatments for tuberculosis and other diseases.

Baltimore established the first citywide system of free libraries in 1886. State lawmakers passed laws restricting child labor in 1894. They passed the first workers' compensation law in 1902. In 1912, the Democratic National Convention was held in Baltimore. It nominated Woodrow Wilson for president.

The United States entered World War I five years later during Wilson's second term as president. More than 62,000 Marylanders served in the armed forces. The U.S. Army established its first training center near the Chesapeake Bay in 1917.

Struggle for Freedom

Prohibition was passed in 1919. It banned the manufacture, sale, and transportation of alcoholic beverages throughout the country. The Maryland state government was opposed to the federal government telling residents what to do. Marylanders were encouraged to defy the law by their own governor, Albert C. Ritchie. Legend has it that this fierce independence earned Maryland the nickname the Free State.

Maryland's African Americans wanted to be free too and have full rights as citizens. The second-oldest chapter of the National Association for the Advancement of Colored People (NAACP) was founded in Baltimore in 1913. Maryland attorney Thurgood Marshall was a leader in the fight for civil rights. In 1954, he won a Supreme Court decision against segregation in public schools. In 1967, President Lyndon Johnson appointed Marshall as the first African American on the Supreme

Thurgood Marshall sits with some of the first African-American students to be integrated into all-white schools.

Maryland

Court. He served on the Court for twenty-four years, retiring in 1991.

Post-War Boom

Some 55,000 Marylanders served in the armed forces during World War II (1939–1945). Many more worked in shipbuilding and other wartime industries. After the war, Maryland's cities and towns grew bigger than ever. But where people lived changed. The black population of the cities increased, while the suburbs attracted more whites. During the Civil War, Baltimore was the third-largest city in the United States. By 1994, it had dropped to the fourteenth-largest city.

These Maryland men worked in shipyards that provided supplies for U.S. troops during World War II.

Despite gains in racial equality, there were still problems. When civil rights leader Martin Luther King Jr. was assassinated in 1968, there were riots in Baltimore, as in other U.S. cities. The governor of Maryland at the time was Spiro T. Agnew. Agnew was a moderate Republican. He improved race relations by expanding the state's antipoverty programs and passing a law for open housing. His efforts earned him the vice president spot on the 1968 Republican ticket. Elected with President Richard Nixon, the two men won re-election in 1972. Soon after, Agnew was accused of corruption while governor and vice president. He was forced to resign in 1973.

Maryland Today

Maryland today is a modern state. Light technology has replaced heavy industry in its cities. In 1980 a new business area called Harborplace opened in Baltimore. Tourists flocked to its shops and restaurants. Other attractions such as the National Aquarium have helped make Baltimore a popular city again. The Old Line State has moved into the twenty-first century with renewed confidence.

Important Dates

1524   Italian explorer Giovanni da Verrazano sails past Chesapeake Bay.

1608   Englishman John Smith explores Chesapeake Bay and maps it.

1631   William Claiborne founds the first permanent settlement on Kent Island.

1634   Leonard Calvert establishes the settlement of St. Mary's City on the Western Shore.

1649   The Act Concerning Religion, one of the first laws granting religious liberty in America, is passed.

1729   The city of Baltimore is founded.

1767   The Mason-Dixon Line is established between Maryland and Pennsylvania. This line divides the North and South.

1774   To protest British taxation patriots in Annapolis burn a British ship carrying tea.

1788   Maryland ratifies the U.S. Constitution on April 28 and becomes the seventh state.

1814   The British attack Maryland during the War of 1812 and in September are defeated in the Battle of Baltimore.

1828   The Baltimore and Ohio Railroad builds the first railway in the United States.

1862   The Battle of Antietam is fought in Sharpsburg on September 17.

1876   Johns Hopkins University is founded in Baltimore.

1913   The National Association for the Advancement of Colored People (NAACP) opens its second chapter in Baltimore.

1917   The U.S. Army establishes the first training center in the United States, near the Chesapeake Bay.

1952   The Chesapeake Bay Bridge opens.

1967   Marylander Thurgood Marshall is appointed to the Supreme Court.

1969   Maryland governor Spiro T. Agnew becomes vice president of the United States.

1980   Harborplace opens in Baltimore and renews the city, bringing many tourists.

1987   Barbara Mikulski becomes the first U.S. woman elected senator in her own right.

1995   James W. Rouse, developer of the planned community of Columbia, Maryland, receives the Presidential Medal of Freedom.

2000   Maryland, Virginia, Pennsylvania, and the District of Columbia sign the Chesapeake Bay Agreement setting standards for the bay's restoration.

Giovanni da Verrazano

Spiro T. Agnew

3 The People

Maryland's population is made up of a range of different people from a variety of countries and cultures. Though nearly 60 percent of the population is made up of Caucasian people, the state's residents come from a wide range of cultures. These include Canadians, Irish, African, Germans, Italians, Koreans, and others from Asia and Latin America. Some have lived in Maryland all their lives, while others are new to the state. No matter how long they have lived in the state, Marylanders' cultures, beliefs, and abilities have helped to shape Maryland and make it the unique state that it is.

People who come from other countries to make Maryland their home often share a part of their culture with other residents. Many businesses that specialize in ethnic foods and other goods offer Marylanders a taste of a culture that is not traditionally typical of the mid-Atlantic states. These stores sometimes open in areas where there are many people of the same culture, or in Maryland's big cities where ethnic populations are especially diverse. Festivals and other cultural celebrations are also held all year long.

Young Marylanders attend a ball game.

Maryland's Native Americans

Before the Europeans came, Native Americans were the only people living on the land that is now Maryland. Unfortunately, many tribes were forced to move as Europeans began to settle in the area. Census numbers for the year 2000 show that less than 1 percent of Maryland's population is Native American.

Before the colonies were established, the Accohannock Tribe lived on the eastern shores of Maryland and Virginia. They are one of Maryland's oldest tribes and are currently trying to obtain federal recognition. This means that they would be able to claim a legal relationship to the United States government and could receive certain federal services.

Every May the tribe holds the Native American Heritage Festival and Powwow. At this event, people can learn about the Accohannock's traditions and culture. The Accohannock also attend powwows in other states and present their culture to schools and other organizations.

African Americans

African Americans are Maryland's largest minority. They make up around 28 percent of the population. A number of African Americans have moved from Washington, D.C., to nearby Prince Georges County in southeastern Maryland. Once mostly white, Prince Georges County is now 63 percent black. Wayne K. Curry is the first African American to hold the county's executive position. He has said that the county is "the only large political subdivison in the nation that went from being all white to a black majority where income and education went up and not down."

Native Americans in Maryland are proud of their heritage and traditions. This youth is dressed in the ceremonial clothing of the Lumbee Indians.

The People

Maryland children attend an art education class at the Baltimore Museum of Art.

Maryland

City of Neighborhoods, Museums, and Music

About nine out of every ten Marylanders live in or near a city. The rest live in rural areas. Annapolis, the state capital, is small. It has only about 36,000 people. Baltimore is the state's largest city with a population of just over 650,000.

Baltimore is known as the city of neighborhoods. Many of these neighborhoods were formed in the 1800's by European immigrants. They wanted to live near people from their homelands. They wanted to be able to speak their native languages and help each other find jobs and places to live.

Many Irish once lived in southwestern Baltimore. They helped build the Baltimore and Ohio railroad in the 1840's. The houses they lived in were supposed to be torn down. However, local residents worked to restore them. The railroad's old engine roundhouse nearby has been turned into a museum. A roundhouse is a circular building that is used for storing and repairing locomotives.

Thomas Ward's father worked for the railroad. "A hundred years from now," he said, "I want tourists to know about the people who lived, worked, worshipped and died here . . ."

Another museum in Baltimore is dedicated to African Americans. The Great Blacks in Wax Museum has more than a hundred life-sized wax figures of famous Maryland African Americans. One of the figures is of Matthew Henson, one of the first explorers to reach the North Pole. The Museum also has a large model of a slave ship.

The National Aquarium in Baltmore has many things to see. The aquarium is seven stories high and has an Atlantic

The National Aquarium in Baltimore has a 225,000 gallon exhibit with sand tiger, lemon, nurse, and sandbar sharks.

coral reef with 335,000 gallons of water and hundreds of tropical reef fish. You can also walk through a South American rain forest encased in glass.

If you like music, there's the Baltimore Symphony Orchestra, which plays classical music. Jazz lovers enjoy live performances at the Eubie Blake Museum and Cultural Center. Eubie Blake was a famous ragtime and jazz composer who lived to be one hundred years old.

A Leader in Education

Learning is important in Maryland. George Washington helped found the first college in the state in 1782. It is called Washington College in his honor. It is the tenth-oldest college in the nation. Mount St. Mary's in Emmitsburg is the country's oldest Catholic college. One of the first U.S. public high schools opened in Baltimore in 1839. Today the city has the oldest all-girls public high school in the country.

> *Only by moving north have I discovered just how deeply South this mid-Atlantic city really is. And it is only in returning as a frequent family visitor through the years that I have discovered the singular pleasures of what natives call Charm City.*
> —writer Diana Cole

Education is an important issue in Maryland.

The People

Famous Marylanders

Benjamin Banneker: Scientist and Writer

Banneker was probably the most famous African American of the 1700s. He was a farmer, a mathematician, an astronomer, an almanac writer, and a surveyor (one who measures the size and position of a piece of land). Thomas Jefferson was impressed by Banneker's abilities and asked him to help survey the new capital in Washington. When the capital's main designer resigned, Banneker was able to reconstruct his plans from memory. "The color of the skin," he wrote in his almanac, "is in no way connected with the strength of the mind."

Edgar Allan Poe: Writer

Poe wasn't born in Maryland but he lived there for several years with his wife. He wrote poetry and horror stories such as "The Tell-Tale Heart" and "The Black Cat." Poe is known as the writer of the first modern detective stories. He died in Baltimore in 1849 and was buried in the city's Westminster Hall and Burying Grounds. Baltimore's professional football team, the Ravens, is named after his most famous poem, "The Raven."

Harriet Tubman: Abolitionist

Harriet Tubman was born into slavery in Maryland in the early 1800s. After escaping to the North, she continued to work for the Underground Railroad to help free many other slaves in Maryland and in other slave states. After the Civil War she settled in New York, where she fought for women's rights and for better living conditions for the elderly and poor.

Babe Ruth: Baseball Player

Born in Baltimore in 1895, George Herman Ruth was one of the greatest baseball players who ever lived. The Sultan of Swat, as he was called, was the first great home-run hitter. Playing for the New York Yankees, he hit 60 home runs in one season. This record was not broken until 1961 by Roger Maris. Ruth hit a total of 714 home runs in his career. His skill and colorful person- ality helped to bring more fans to baseball than ever before.

Billie Holiday: Singer

Billie Holiday was one of America's great jazz singers. She was born in Baltimore and later moved to New York where she began to sing in local clubs. By the time she was eighteen, Holiday had recorded her first record. Musicians respected her ability to express the pain and loneliness in her life through her singing, and called her Lady Day. In her later years, Holiday was addicted to drugs and alcohol, but she kept singing almost up until her death at age forty-four.

Barbara Mikulski: Politician

Barbara Mikulski is the first woman to serve in both houses of the U.S. Congress. In 1976 she was elected to the U.S. House of Representatives, where she served four terms before becoming a senator. She has been a U.S. senator from Maryland since 1987 and is the first woman to win a senate seat not previously held by a husband. Senator Mikulski takes a liberal view on social issues and is a leader on issues of women's health care.

The U.S. Naval Academy in Annapolis was established in 1845. Today it is an undergraduate college for men and women who want to serve in the navy or marine corps.

Annapolis is home of the U.S. Naval Academy. Cadets spend their summers training on ships at sea. When they graduate, each cadet becomes an officer in the navy or marine corps.

The University of Maryland, Baltimore County, has a special program for African-American students. Dr. Freeman A. Hrabowski, the college president, has been called the Pied Piper of the smart students. He instructs fifty black students a year in math and science. The school has no football team, but it has a chess team. They have their own pep rallies.

Sports and Recreation

Marylanders like to work and study. But they like to play too. The state is home to the Baltimore Orioles baseball team and the Baltimore Ravens football team.

Annapolis's beautiful harbor is one of the East's top centers for sailboating. Visitors can sail aboard the schooner

Woodwind, a classic replica of a luxury yacht from the early 1900s. During their tour of the harbor, amateur sailors can help the crew raise the sails or even take turns steering the ship.

One of the state's most popular sports—lacrosse—is the oldest team sport in North America. It was invented by Native Americans. Each player uses a stick with a net attached at one end to throw a ball into the opposite team's goal. Johns Hopkins University and the University of Maryland have two of the best college lacrosse teams.

Schooners have many sails and are usually large enough to have living quarters built in for comfort.

Maryland's state sport is jousting. This sport developed in the Middle Ages when knights on horseback tried to knock each other to the ground with long lances (metal-tipped wooden spears). Marylanders play a less violent form of jousting. Riders attempt to "spear" hanging rings with a lance. Each rider must do this while galloping on horseback. The one who lifts the most rings is the champion. Marylanders have enjoyed jousting since colonial times.

Jousting tournaments are held throughout the state.

Maryland

Helping Others

Maryland, like every state, has problems of poverty, homelessness, and racial prejudice. Young people get to talk about these problems and what they can do about them in a unique program. It is sponsored by the Washington Institute for Jewish Leadership and Values in Rockville, Maryland. The program is called *Panim el Panim,* which means Face to Face in Hebrew. Teenagers from around the nation come here for four days to discuss social issues with political and religious leaders.

In one session, the teens met a homeless person who told them about her life. "She shattered our stereotypes of street people as uneducated vagrants," said Sarah Jordan.

"In this program, the kids meet [people] who are really interested in what they have to say," says Rabbi Sid Schwarz, president of the institute. "As a result, teens come to realize that our American political system is open to those who take the time to educate themselves about the issues and care enough to become involved."

Calendar of Events

Maple Syrup Heritage Festival

Every year this March festival is held in Thurmont. Visitors can enjoy tree-tapping and sap-boiling demonstrations, storytelling, and other activities.

The Maryland International Kite Exposition

This event is held in April in Ocean City. It features kites of all kinds, colors, and sizes. Among the many contests are a stunt kite championship and a kite makers' competition.

The Preakness Celebration

The Preakness Stakes is held in Baltimore every May at Pimlico Race Course. It is one of the most famous horse races in the country. Other events include parades, races, concerts, and fireworks.

The Montgomery County International Festival

Formerly known as the Montgomery County Ethnic Heritage Festival, this one-day event is held in June in Wheaton. More than eighty different ethnic groups who have settled there celebrate their heritage with crafts, foods, and entertainment. Visitors can watch a Cambodian dance troupe or listen to an Irish band.

Fiddle and Banjo Contest

Held in July in Friendsville, this friendly competition features not only musicians playing traditional country and bluegrass music, but also clog and buck-and-wing dancers.

Fiddling at a competition

56

The Maryland State Fair

For eleven days in August, Timonium hosts this event, which includes livestock shows, rides, arts and crafts, horse racing, and contests. At the birthing center, visitors can see local farmers' cows and pigs give birth to their young.

Skipjack Race and Festival

During Labor Day weekend, many people gather on Deal Island for this event. Activities include arts and crafts, contests, and the annual skipjack races, honoring the official state boat. A skipjack is a small boat with one mast and a V-shaped bottom.

Skipjacks

The National Hard Crab Derby

This September celebration in Crisfield includes crab-cooking and crab-picking contests, a plastic boat regatta, and, of course, the crab derby. In the derby, crabs with their shells numbered race each other across the ground.

The State Jousting Championship

Held in Tuckahoe State Park in October, this event has men, women, and children competing in ring tournaments in colorful costumes. Thousands of fans come to cheer for their favorites.

4 How It Works

Government is the system by which a state is run. The government makes laws for its residents and enforces them. Maryland's government listens to its citizens. Government leaders have often been independent thinkers.

Local Government

Maryland is divided into twenty-three counties. In each county, one city or town is the county seat. Elected officials meet there to make local county laws. City councils or county commissioners enforce the laws. The county government runs some towns and cities that are unincorporated. An unincorporated community is not self-governing. It does not have its own police department and other services and must rely on the county to provide these. Towns and cities that are incorporated are run by their own governments.

Baltimore, Maryland's largest city, is not part of a county. It is an independent city run by a mayor and a city council. That is very unusual. Only one other state has cities that are independent of a county.

An aerial view of Maryland's capital, Annapolis

At the end of the Revolutionary War, George Washington resigned his commission—or stepped down as Commander-in-Chief—at the Maryland State House.

Annapolis—A Capital City

Annapolis has been Maryland's capital since 1694. "In a few years it will probably be one of the best built cities in America," one English visitor wrote in 1769. It is one of the oldest state capitals. The governor lives here, and the general assembly meets in the State House each January for a period of ninety days.

Annapolis's State House is the oldest continually used state house in the nation.

Annapolis was the nation's capital for a very short time—from November 1783 to June 1784. After that, the capital was moved to New York and later to several other cities. In 1789, Maryland and Virginia gave land for a permanent capital city, Washington.

Maryland's official state song is "Maryland, My Maryland." You might recognize its tune. It's a German Christmas carol, "O Tannenbaum," also known as "O Christmas Tree."

Branches of Government

Executive The governor is head of the executive branch. He or she executes laws and appoints people to high office. The governor is elected to a four-year term. He or she can only serve two terms in a row.

Legislative This branch makes the state's laws. It is called the General Assembly. It is divided into two parts. The Senate has 47 members and the House of Delegates has 141 members. All General Assembly members are elected to four-year terms.

Judicial The judicial branch interprets the laws. It also enforces them. When a person is accused of breaking a law, he or she goes on trial in one of twelve district or eight circuit courts. If someone is found guilty, the case can be appealed before the court of special appeals. If he or she is found guilty again, the person can take the case to the court of appeals. This is the highest court in the state with seven judges. Unlike many states, Maryland does not have a supreme court.

How a Bill Becomes a Law

Have you ever wondered how laws are made? They often start out as the ideas of the state's residents. When residents think of new laws they can contact their state representatives. The representatives then write up a proposal called a bill. The bill is presented to the president of the state's house of delegates who then assigns the bill to a committee. It is the committee's responsibility to hold a hearing when the bill is discussed. If the committee members vote and approve the bill, it is sent back to the house. All members of the house of delegates vote for or against the bill. Once the bill is approved by the house, it goes to the state senate to be discussed and debated again. When the

Star-shaped Fort McHenry is a national monument and historic shrine.

senate approves the bill, it is then presented to the governor. He or she has the option to sign the bill or veto—reject—it. If the governor signs it, the bill officially becomes a state law. Even if the governor vetoes the bill, it still has a chance to become a law. The rejected bill goes back to the house and senate for a new vote. Two-thirds of the house and senate can vote to overturn the veto. If this happens the bill becomes a law.

Getting Involved

Lawmakers aren't the only ones who have a say in Maryland's government. Private citizens can do more than suggest ideas to their representatives and vote in elections. They can form citizens' groups and other organizations for change. Many people in Maryland are worried about the future. They see the state getting more and more crowded. New homes and developments are taking up remaining open space. This space could be used for parks and other recreational areas.

Each one of us can make a difference but together we can bring about change.
—Senator Barbara Mikulski

In 1996, people who were concerned about Maryland's future got together. They didn't want their state to lose all its open land to homes and businesses, so they formed a group called 1,000

Friends of Maryland. The group included business people and environmental groups. They say their mission is "to preserve what is best about Maryland and to encourage sensible growth." The group wants Maryland to fix up existing neigh-

If you live in Maryland and have a concern or want to express your opinion about an issue that affects your community, go to the Maryland Electronic Capital Web site at http://www.mec.state.md.us. Then go to the "Getting Things Done in Maryland" page. From there go to "Contact General Assembly" page. Finally, go to the "Contact a Legislator" page. Here you can follow the easy steps to send an e-mail to any state legislator.

borhoods instead of tearing them down. It wants to see government carefully plan new communities. It also cares about the environment. In April 2000, it filed a suit against the Environmental Protection Agency (EPA). The group believes the EPA's acceptable level of emissions (gas released into the air) from cars should be lowered.

The people of Maryland have friends to help protect their rights—a thousand of them.

Maryland's residents are very serious about protecting the environment.

5 Making a Living

Making a living in Maryland can be hard work. But most Marylanders aren't complaining. In 2000, Maryland residents earned the sixth-highest incomes in the nation.

What do they do? About 80 percent of Marylanders work in hotels, restaurants, hospitals, resorts, museums, universities, and other service industries. Many of them serve tourists who spend more than $6 billion yearly in the state.

Other Marylanders work in trading. Foreign goods come and go in the big port of Baltimore. Still other people hold government jobs. This isn't surprising since Washington, D.C., is a short distance away. Some government workers don't have to leave Maryland for their work. They have jobs in medical research at the National Institutes of Health in Bethesda. Others are involved in aerospace research at the Goddard Space

The Chesapeake Bay Bridge was built from 1949 to 1952 to link the Eastern Shore to the rest of Maryland. It made traveling much easier within the state and has increased the exchange of goods and services. The Bay Bridge is 4.3 miles long from shore to shore and is one of the world's longest bridges.

This Maryland girl is selling homegrown tomatoes at her family's roadside stand in Princess Anne.

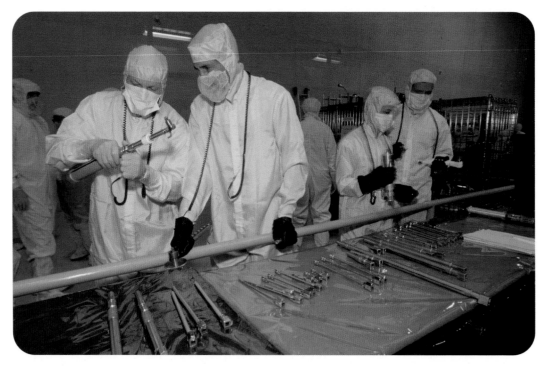

These astronauts are testing tools that will be used in space. They are wearing special clothes to keep the high-tech equipment clean.

Flight Center in Greenbelt. Some Marylanders work at the headquarters of the Social Security Administration (SSA) in Baltimore. The SSA gives money to older Americans and people who are disabled.

Agriculture

Tobacco was once the most important crop in Maryland. In 1698, the minister Hugh Jones of Calvert County wrote, "Tobacco is our meat, drink, clothing and monies." This is no longer true.

There are fewer than a thousand tobacco farms left in the southern part of the state. As more Americans understand the harmful effects of smoking cigarettes, tobacco sales are falling. The state has a special program to stop tobacco farming. It is giving money to tobacco farmers over a ten-year period. This will give the farmers time to experiment with other crops, such as flowers, organic vegetables, and hay.

In ten years, tobacco farming may be little more than a memory.

Flowers and shrubs are the leading crops in Maryland today. Corn, soybeans, and wheat are also important. Orchards in western Maryland produce apples, peaches, pears, and other fruit.

Many flowers and shrubs that are grown in Maryland are sent to stores around the state and across the country.

Chickens are the main livestock. More than three million chickens are kept for egg laying. Three hundred million, however, are raised for eating. These chickens are called broilers. Have you ever seen chicken with a "Perdue" label? These chickens come from the largest chicken farm in Maryland. Perdue Farms started out as a family business and is now the fourth-largest chicken farm in the world.

Shell Fishing

Maryland shell fishers, known as watermen, harvest more oysters than fishers in any other state. The Chesapeake Bay is also famous for its blue crabs. Steamed, sautéed, or cooked in small

Maryland is famous for its crabs. Visitors from around the country come to the state to enjoy these crustaceans.

Catching crabs by hand can be fun on a warm, sunny day.

crab cakes or soup, the blue crab is one of Maryland's favorite dishes. Native crab lovers claim its meat is tastier than lobster. Marylanders think so much of their favorite shellfish that in 1989 they named it the state crustacean (shellfish). The shellfish are even in a favorite state slogan: "Maryland is for crabs."

Professional crabbers go out into Chesapeake Bay in their skipjacks. They catch the blue crabs in crab pots. The crab enters a trap in the pot and cannot get out again.

People who catch crabs for fun may prefer the old-fashioned long-handled dip net. You wade into the water and when you see a crab, you dip the net to catch it.

Many crabbers also use a hand line, or bait line. A long string or fishing line with a weight attached to the bottom and bait—often chicken necks—are tied to the line, which is lowered into the water until it reaches the bottom. When a crab begins to nibble on the bait the line is pulled up slowly, and the crab is scooped up with a net.

Made in Maryland

Only about one out of ten workers in Maryland has a job in manufacturing. However, this is an important part of the state's economy. The largest number of the state's manufacturers package foods. Maryland companies and canneries process everything from seafood to chicken parts.

Your kitchen spice rack may be filled with spices made by McCormick and Company. This spice company in Sparks, Maryland, has been in business for more than one hundred years. The company was started by twenty-five-year-old Willoughby McCormick in a room and cellar in Baltimore. He sold his first products door-to-door, and they included such items as root beer, fruit syrups, and a product called Iron Glue. McCormick claimed it "Sticks Everything But the Buyer."

Mining is a small industry in Maryland. The state once produced a large amount of coal for fuel. The level of coal produced today is much lower, partly because the demand for coal is less. The top minerals mined today include sand and gravel. Sand is used to make concrete. Gravel is used to build roads and landing strips for airfields.

Many other products are made in Maryland. Steel and aluminum are produced in the state. Sparrows Point is one of the nation's leading centers for building and repairing ships. Aircraft and high-tech electronics such as computers have become important. Interstate 270 in Montgomery County is often called the state's high-technology corridor.

Many things we use and eat every day are made in Maryland. And it makes Marylanders proud.

Maryland

These workers need to wear protective gear so that they will not get burned while pouring melted aluminum.

Products & Resources

Chickens

These birds are one of Maryland's most important agricultural products. The state produces over three hundred million chickens every year.

Power tools

The Black & Decker Tool Company, head-quartered in Towson, has been making tools of all kinds since 1915.

Steel

The iron ore used to make steel at Sparrows Point, near Baltimore, comes all the way from Canada and Venezuela in South America. The Bethlehem Steel plant at Sparrows Point is one of the world's largest steel mills. It supplies steel and steel products nationwide.

Fishing

Maryland's fishing industry produces more than $50 million in sales each year. Striped bass, white perch, and menhaden are three kinds of fish caught in the Chesapeake Bay. Shark, bluefish, and flounder are harvested off the Atlantic coast.

Tourism

Tourism is a big business in Maryland. Baltimore alone—with its museums, fine restaurants, and exciting nightlife—pulls in close to five million visitors every year.

Chemical Products

Fertilizer is one of the leading chemical products made in Maryland. Other important chemical products are soap and paint.

By learning how to respect and protect all of Maryland's resources, these students are helping to ensure a bright and prosperous future for their state.

Maryland

Saving the Environment

The people of this state are not proud of the pollution. Waste from factories and sewage systems runs into rivers and the Chesapeake Bay, killing thousands of fish. Overfishing and illegal fishing of fish that are too young also hurt the fishing industry. Maryland and neighboring Virginia, Pennsylvania, and Washington, D.C., have formed the Chesapeake Bay Program. The goal of this program is to clean up local waters. Open space is gradually disappearing in Maryland. The state and federal governments are working to save the land left

We are probably 10 to 15 years ahead of any other large-scale ecosystem restoration dealing with water pollution. What we do over the course of the next five to ten years will likely become the model for the Mississippi River and Gulf of Mexico.
—J. Charles Fox, senior policy adviser for the Chesapeake Bay Foundation

around Baltimore and nearby Washington, D.C. They want to preserve this land for parks and other recreational areas.

Maryland is a state with a proud past, a busy present, and an exciting future. From the Chesapeake Bay in the east to the Allegheny Mountains in the west, Maryland is a state worth treasuring.

The state flag is divided into four sections. The two black-and-gold sections represent the coat of arms of the Calvert family. The Calverts led the first English families who settled in Maryland. The red-and-white sections of the flag represent the Crossland coat of arms. Crossland was the family name of the mother of the first Lord Baltimore, George Calvert. The flag was officially adopted in 1904.

The front side of the state seal shows an armored Lord Baltimore on a horse. However, it is the back side of the seal that is used for official purposes. The back of the seal shows a farmer and a fisherman holding a shield with the Calvert and Crossland coats of arms.

Maryland

Maryland, My Maryland

Words by James R. Randall
Music: "Oh, Tannenbaum"

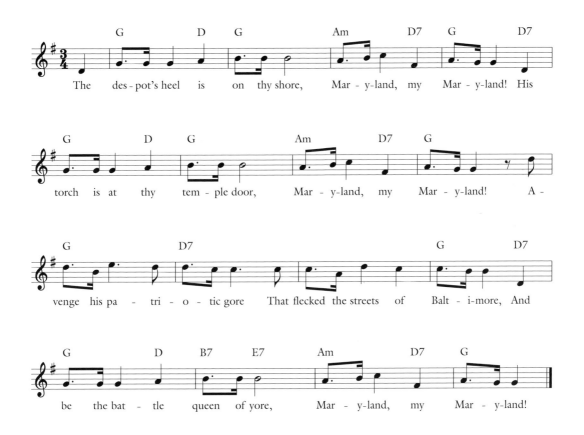

More About Maryland

Books

Burgan, Michael. *Maryland*. Danbury, CT: Children's Press, 1999.

Fradin, Dennis Brindell. *The Maryland Colony.* Danbury, CT: Children's Press, 1990.

Johnston, Joyce. *Maryland*. Minneapolis, MN: Lerner Publications, 1997.

Kummer, Patricia K. *Maryland*. Mankato, MN: Capstone Press, 1998.

Thompson, Kathleen. *Maryland*. Austin, TX: Raintree-Steck Vaughn, 1996.

Wanning, Esther. *Maryland: The Spirit of America*. New York: Harry N. Abrams, 1998.

Web sites

Maryland's Kids' Page:

http://www.sos.state.md.us/sos/kids/html/kidhome.html

Maryland's Department of Natural Resources for Kids:

http://www.dnr.state.md.us/mydnr

About the Author

Steve Otfinoski has written more than ninety fiction and non-fiction books for young readers. His previous works for Marshall Cavendish include the twelve-volume transportation series for early readers, *Here We Go*!, and books on New Hampshire and Georgia in the Celebrate the States series.

Mr. Otfinoski is also a playwright and has his own theater company, History Alive!, that brings plays about American history to schoolchildren. He lives with his wife, Beverly, and their two children in Connecticut.

Index

Page numbers in **boldface** are illustrations.